FRANCIS FRITH'S

# ODIHAM
## THEN & NOW

### PHOTOGRAPHIC MEMORIES

**SHEILA MILLARD,** a former Civil Service librarian, initially lived in Odiham from 1972-74, returning in 1982 after living abroad for eight years. She was a member of the Odiham Society Executive Committee for 18 years and is now the Society's Vice President, as well as continuing as Archivist and Editor of the Society's bi-annual Journal. In 2002 she received an Award of Merit from Hart District Council for service to the community. She has written numerous articles covering local history for the Hampshire Field Club Newsletter and the Odiham Society Journal. This is her third book of local historical interest.

# FRANCIS FRITH'S
# PHOTOGRAPHIC MEMORIES

# ODIHAM
## THEN & NOW

### PHOTOGRAPHIC MEMORIES

## SHEILA MILLARD

First published in the United Kingdom in 2004 by
Frith Book Company Ltd

Limited Hardback Subscribers Edition Published in 2004
ISBN 1-85937-833-1

Paperback Edition 2004
ISBN 1-85937-834-X

British Library Cataloguing in Publication Data

Francis Frith's Odiham, Then and Now
Photographic Memories
Sheila Millard

Frith Book Company Ltd
Frith's Barn, Teffont,
Salisbury, Wiltshire SP3 5QP
Tel: +44 (0) 1722 716 376
Email: info@francisfrith.co.uk
www.francisfrith.co.uk

Printed and bound in Great Britain

Front Cover: **HIGH STREET** *c1950* O8007
Frontispiece: **THE GEORGE HOTEL** *1924* 75277

*The colour-tinting is for illustrative purposes only, and is not intended
to be historically accurate*

Acknowledgements
Line drawings by R. S. Millard. © Sheila Millard.
2004 Photographs by Julian Hight.

# CONTENTS

# Acknowledgements

The author is most grateful to the following for the assistance they have
given her in the preparation of this book:
The Earl of Malmesbury, Edward Roberts, Dorothy Crocker,
Constance Barker, Chris Riley, Betty Goddard, Tad Champion,
Mark Forrester, Joan Warren, Cicely Anscombe and in particular to
Trish Paton for her patience and skill in the preparation of the text.

# FRANCIS FRITH
## VICTORIAN PIONEER

FRANCIS FRITH, founder of the world-famous photographic archive, was a complex and multi-talented man. A devout Quaker and a highly successful Victorian businessman, he was philosophical by nature and pioneering in outlook.

By 1855 he had already established a wholesale grocery business in Liverpool, and sold it for the astonishing sum of £200,000, which is the equivalent today of over £15,000,000. Now a very rich man, he was able to indulge his passion for travel. As a child he had pored over travel books written by early explorers, and his fancy and imagination had been stirred by family holidays to the sublime mountain regions of Wales and Scotland. 'What lands of spirit-stirring and enriching scenes and places!' he had written. He was to return to these scenes of grandeur in later years to 'recapture the thousands of vivid and tender memories', but with a different purpose. Now in his thirties, and captivated by the new science of photography, Frith set out on a series of pioneering journeys up the Nile and to the Near East that occupied him from 1856 until 1860.

### INTRIGUE AND EXPLORATION

These far-flung journeys were packed with intrigue and adventure. In his life story, written when he was sixty-three, Frith tells of being held captive by bandits, and of fighting 'an awful midnight battle to the very point of surrender with a deadly pack of hungry, wild dogs'. Wearing flowing Arab costume, Frith arrived at Akaba by camel sixty years before Lawrence of Arabia, where he encountered 'desert princes and rival sheikhs, blazing with jewel-hilted swords'.

He was the first photographer to venture beyond the sixth cataract of the Nile. Africa was still the mysterious 'Dark Continent', and Stanley and Livingstone's historic meeting was a decade into the future. The conditions for picture taking confound belief. He laboured for hours in his wicker dark-room in the sweltering heat of the desert, while the volatile chemicals fizzed dangerously in their trays. Back in London he exhibited his photographs and was 'rapturously cheered' by members of the Royal Society. His reputation as a photographer was made overnight.

### VENTURE OF A LIFE-TIME

Characteristically, Frith quickly spotted the opportunity to create a new business as a specialist publisher of photographs. He lived in an era of immense and sometimes violent change.

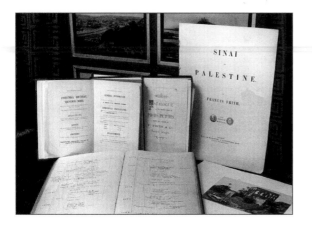

For the poor in the early part of Victoria's reign work was exhausting and the hours long, and people had precious little free time to enjoy themselves. Most had no transport other than a cart or gig at their disposal, and rarely travelled far beyond the boundaries of their own town or village. However, by the 1870s the railways had threaded their way across the country, and Bank Holidays and half-day Saturdays had been made obligatory by Act of Parliament. All of a sudden the working man and his family were able to enjoy days out and see a little more of the world.

With typical business acumen, Francis Frith foresaw that these new tourists would enjoy having souvenirs to commemorate their days out. In 1860 he married Mary Ann Rosling and set out on a new career: his aim was to photograph every city, town and village in Britain. For the next thirty years he travelled the country by train and by pony and trap, producing fine photographs of seaside resorts and beauty spots that were keenly bought by millions of Victorians. These prints were painstakingly pasted into family albums and pored over during the dark nights of winter, rekindling precious memories of summer excursions.

## THE RISE OF FRITH & CO

Frith's studio was soon supplying retail shops all over the country. To meet the demand he gathered about him a small team of photographers, and published the work of independent artist-photographers of the calibre of Roger Fenton and Francis Bedford. In order to gain some understanding of the scale of Frith's business one only has to look at the catalogue issued by Frith & Co in 1886: it runs to some 670 pages, listing not only many thousands of views of the British Isles but also many photographs of most European countries, and China, Japan, the USA and Canada - note the sample page shown on page 9 from the hand-written Frith & Co ledgers recording the pictures. By 1890 Frith had created the greatest specialist photographic publishing company in the world, with over 2,000 sales outlets - more than the combined number that Boots and WH Smith have today! The picture on the next page shows the Frith & Co display board at Ingleton in the Yorkshire Dales (left of window). Beautifully constructed with a mahogany frame and gilt inserts, it could display up to a dozen local scenes.

## POSTCARD BONANZA

The ever-popular holiday postcard we know today took many years to develop. In 1870 the Post Office issued the first plain cards, with a pre-printed stamp on one face. In 1894 they allowed other publishers' cards to be sent through the mail with an attached adhesive halfpenny stamp. Demand grew rapidly, and in 1895 a new size of postcard was permitted called the court card, but there was little room for illustration. In 1899, a year after Frith's death, a new card measuring 5.5 x 3.5 inches became the standard format, but it was not until 1902 that the divided back came into being, so that the address and message could be on one face and a full-size illustration on the other. Frith & Co were in the vanguard of postcard development: Frith's sons Eustace and Cyril continued their father's monumental task, expanding the number of views offered to the public and recording more and more places in Britain, as the

coasts and countryside were opened up to mass travel.

Francis Frith had died in 1898 at his villa in Cannes, his great project still growing. The archive he created continued in business for another seventy years. By 1970 it contained over a third of a million pictures showing 7,000 British towns and villages.

## FRANCIS FRITH'S LEGACY

Frith's legacy to us today is of immense significance and value, for the magnificent archive of evocative photographs he created provides a unique record of change in the cities, towns and villages throughout Britain over a century and more. Frith and his fellow studio photographers revisited locations many times down the years to update their views, compiling for us an enthralling and colourful pageant of British life and character.

We are fortunate that Frith was dedicated to recording the minutiae of everyday life. For it is this sheer wealth of visual data, the painstaking chronicle of changes in dress, transport, street layouts, buildings, housing, engineering and landscape that captivates us so much today. His remarkable images offer us a powerful link with the past and with the lives of our ancestors.

## THE VALUE OF THE ARCHIVE TODAY

Computers have now made it possible for Frith's many thousands of images to be accessed almost instantly. Frith's images are increasingly used as visual resources, by social historians, by researchers into genealogy and ancestry, by architects and town planners, and by teachers involved in local history projects.

In addition, the archive offers every one of us an opportunity to examine the places where we and our families have lived and worked down the years. Highly successful in Frith's own era, the archive is now, a century and more on, entering a new phase of popularity. Historians consider the Francis Frith Collection to be of prime national importance. It is the only archive of its kind remaining in private ownership. Francis Frith's archive is now housed in an historic timber barn in the beautiful village of Teffont in Wiltshire. Its founder would not recognize the archive office as it is today. In place of the many thousands of dusty boxes containing glass plate negatives and an all-pervading odour of photographic chemicals, there are now ranks of computer screens. He would be amazed to watch his images travelling round the world at unimaginable speeds through internet lines.

The archive's future is both bright and exciting. Francis Frith, with his unshakeable belief in making photographs available to the greatest number of people, would undoubtedly approve of what is being done today with his lifetime's work. His photographs depicting our shared past are now bringing pleasure and enlightenment to millions around the world a century and more after his death.

# ODIHAM
## THEN AND NOW
## AN INTRODUCTION

The Old House

ODIHAM is situated on the north-facing slope of the chalk downs where they meet the clay and gravels of north-east Hampshire. The parish, which includes North Warnborough, covers 5,787 acres, including 600 acres of common land.

Held by King Harold before the Norman Conquest, Odiham remained a royal manor until 1603. Archaeological evidence has been found of Bronze Age / Early Iron Age and Romano-British settlements. The rectilinear shape of the settlement was constrained to the north of the High Street by the formerly heavily wooded deer park covering some 500 acres, and to the south by the common fields. Modern developments have been mainly restricted to the eastern and western outskirts.

Odiham is almost unique in that over the centuries there has been no change to its street pattern. Medieval alleyways still connect the High Street to The Bury, where to the south it is

**FROM THE CHURCH TOWER** *1906* 55851

thought that there was once an Anglo-Saxon residence. The regularity of the size of the property plots in the High Street suggests that Odiham was a 'new town', perhaps founded by King John.

## The Bury

The word Bury derives from 'bearth', meaning 'a hill or mound', possibly defended, and this, the higher part of the town, is considered to have been the original area of settlement. Traditionally, from the mid 15th century fairs were held here and in the High Street on mid-Lent Saturday, the Cherry Fair was held here in July - an indication of Odiham's commercial importance during the Middle Ages. During the 19th century the fairs specialised in horses, cattle and toys; they were officially abolished in 1895, although they continued to a lesser degree until just before the Second World War. The Bury has been the venue for more recent festivals commemorating historical events, and carol-singing takes place here at Christmas.

## All Saints' Church

The present church, which is one of the two mentioned under the entry for Odiham in the *Domesday Book*, is believed to have replaced earlier buildings on this site. A Saxon bone was discovered during restoration of the north wall of the present building, parts of which are over 900 years old. It is the largest parish church in the north of the diocese, and in 1851, when the old square box pews were removed, the new open seats and galleries could accommodate 1,200 parishioners. It has been described as 'an illustrated history of church architecture'.

## The Almshouses

The parish of Odiham is fortunate to be richly endowed with charitable bequests dating from the early 17th century. Prior to their amalgamation in 1886, fourteen different charitable funds were separately administered. These and subsequent bequests are now managed by the fifteen Trustees of the Odiham Consolidated Charities, who are responsible for the provision and the maintenance of the almshouses and the relief of need in the parish.

## Robert May's School

Robert May's Grammar School closed in 1951 and reopened in 1987 as Robert May's Secondary Modern School. The building was renamed Mayhill Junior School in 1975 when Robert May's Comprehensive School in West Street opened.

## Cemetery Hill and King Street

King Street was previously known as King's Barn Lane and then Burgess Lane - the Burgess family owned property in the vicinity, which by the mid 19th century had been acquired by the King family's Odiham Brewery. The entrance to the cemetery is at the top of the hill.

## The High Street

Rarely now can one appreciate an uncluttered aspect of this much admired long, wide, gently winding street. However, the view was also blocked prior to the late 18th century - not by vehicles, but by a market house and shambles (permanent market stalls) situated in the middle of the street between the George and King Street. They would have been demolished to cope with the increase of coach traffic after the advent of the turnpikes.

Odiham High Street has the finest range of historic buildings of any town in Hampshire. Dating from 1300, they are nearly all listed, and their setting and the special character of the street is further protected by its designation as a Conservation Area. Prior to Georgian and Victorian 'modernisation', at least 20 of the timber-framed buildings were jettied (in other words, they had an overhanging upper storey). A glance at the side walls of some of the buildings gives an indication of their earlier origins.

Through the analysis of tree-ring patterns it is possible to determine the date at which a timber-framed building was constructed. A programme of dendrochronology (tree-ring dating) funded by Hampshire County Council, The Odiham Society and individual property owners has provided a definitive building date for eight of the High Street properties. These dates provide an insight into the development of the High Street; moreover, the size and quality of the buildings are indications of the wealth and pros-perity of Odiham in the medieval period. Did the craftsmen working on the frequent additions and repairs to Odiham Castle build these houses with the timber and on land granted by successive monarchs to their loyal servants?

The High Street still retains the mix of houses and shops that it had in medieval times, although the doubling of the population of Odiham Parish between 1784 and 1831 brought about changes to its appearance. Several of the larger houses were divided to meet the increased demand for accommodation. The former stalls and the boards let down from windows on market and fair days were being replaced by permanent shop windows. The tradesmen, whose wares were largely prepared or manufactured on site, increased from 44 to 60. In contrast, by the early 20th century (when the earlier photographs in this book were taken) the population of the parish had dropped by some 300, and the number of tradesmen in the High Street had reduced by half.

One hundred years on there are even greater contrasts. The residential population has

The Bridewell, Odiham

reduced by nearly a third, although the number of houses has increased by the conversion to residential use of former workshops, stables, coach houses and so on situated at the rear of properties fronting the High Street, and by building on former garden plots. But set against this are the previously divided houses that have been restored back to one dwelling; also, today very few of the shopkeepers and their families now live above the shop. These upper storeys, together with some of the larger houses where residential staff would have been employed, and a large public house, have all been converted to office use. In line with national trends, a former inn and five shops have become restaurants. The High Street is still a commercial centre for the surrounding area, and there are currently ten shops, including banks and a post office, which cater for everyday requirements.

**The Chalk Pit**

It has been estimated that some half a million tons of chalk has been removed from this pit. The Odiham area is the eastern extremity for the use of reconstructed chalk for building in southern England.

**Colt Hill**

This area, to the east of the former royal deer park, takes its name from the horse stud established in 1223-24 to breed horses for use in the Plantagenet Wars. The last reference to this stud was in 1361, when Edward III ordered that all horses, mares and studs in his royal parks should be sold; the proceeds were to go towards repairs to Windsor Castle.

**The Basingstoke Canal**

Opened in 1794, this 37 miles of waterway from its junction with the River Wey navigation at West Byfleet linked Basingstoke with London. It was built with the intention of boosting local trade by providing cheap transport for agricultural goods and locally produced timber, bricks and chalk. However, the canal's construction costs were twice the estimate, and it was never commercially viable. The shareholders did not receive a dividend, and ironically a prosperous period in the late 1830s was when the canal carried materials for the construction of the London to Southampton Railway; the opening of the railway in 1839 to Winchfield resulted in the bankruptcy of the original canal company. Another lucrative period in the 1850s was in connection with the building of Aldershot military camp; the last commercial craft, carrying timber, operated in 1950.

The Surrey and Hampshire Canal Society was formed in 1966 to campaign for the canal's restoration and public ownership. This goal was achieved when Surrey and Hampshire County Councils purchased it in 1974, and restoration work began in earnest. It was officially re-opened in 1991, and the canal is again navigable from Greywell Tunnel to the River Wey. The '*John Pinkerton*', designed to resemble a canal narrow-boat and named after the engineer responsible for the canal's construction, operates through the Odiham reach during the summer.

The importance of the immediate environs of the canal is recognised by their designation as a SSSI for nature conservation, and as a conservation area to protect them from intrusive development.

The New Inn was renamed the Waterwitch by the brewers in 1976. The name commemorates a narrow-boat which traded on the canal towards the end of the 19th century.

## North Warnborough

A former tithing, North Warnborough is part of Odiham Parish. It too has numerous fine timber-framed listed buildings, the earliest dating from 1368-69. The Basingstoke Canal and the River Whitewater flow through the village, and on the latter there were fulling and corn mills. Odiham Castle was built in a loop of the River Whitewater; although it is known locally as King John's Castle, archaeological investigations have found remains of earlier buildings dating from c1100. King John was a frequent visitor, and left from here to sign the Magna Carta at Runnymede.

## Greywell

Greywell to the west is mainly a farming community, and a large part of it is woodland. Formerly there were hop gardens here, and peat was dug on the moors (now Greywell Fen, owned by the Hampshire and Isle of Wight Wildlife Trust). Greywell Mill on the River Whitewater ground corn and beans before its closure in 1933. A pumping station was built in 1911, which before mechanisation provided employment locally. The Basingstoke Canal passes under Greywell Hill in a tunnel nearly a mile long. This partially collapsed in 1932, and is now a SSSI as a bat refuge.

## Dogmersfield

Dogmersfield lies to the north east of Odiham. The original medieval village was dispersed by Sir Henry Mildmay (Ellis St John's grandson) in 1792 when the surrounding park was enclosed. Sir Henry also ensured that the Basingstoke Canal was built around the park, which then covered some 1000 acres. The St John and Mildmay families were also lords of the manor of Odiham from 1742. The house and part of the estate was sold in 1933, and passed through a succession of owners and uses until 1981, when a fire gutted the building. It was restored in 1983, and is now being converted into a hotel.

## Long Sutton

Long Sutton, to the south of Odiham, straddles one of England's oldest routes - the Harrow Way. It used to be called Sheeps Sutton, the name reflecting the former sheep pastures of the surrounding downs. Lord Wandsworth College, set in 1200 acres of farmland, was built in 1915 as a boarding school for orphan boys from an agricultural background. The magnificent gates were built in 1920 in a style reminiscent of those at the entrance to World War I cemeteries.

**HIGH STREET** *1906* 53714

# THE BURY, THE CHURCH, CEMETERY HILL AND KING STREET

**THE PARISH CHURCH AND THE STOCKS** *1906* 55853

All Saints' Church dominates the south side of The Bury. The seven-day clock on the tower (by John More & Sons of Clerkenwell) was purchased by public subscription in 1874. Glimpsed through the trees in the churchyard is the tabletop tomb of Robert May, founder of Odiham Grammar School, whose spire can be seen on the left. The stocks and whipping post were re-sited here in 1905. The brick building beside the church gate is the stable block of Bury House, which in 1901 was owned by the parish and housed the parish fire engine.

15

► **THE STOCKS** *1903* 49207

A four-hour period in the stocks was the usual reward for
misdemeanours such as blasphemy, drunkenness,
vagrancy or breaking the Sabbath. The whipping post has
iron manacles of three different sizes to fit all comers!
They are shown here against the northern wall of the
Bridewell in The Bury, which was purpose-built in 1743 as
a prison or house of correction; by 1847 it had become a
police station.

The Bridewell, Odiham

▲ **THE STOCKS AND WHIPPING POST** *2004* O8743

The stocks and whipping post were moved from their previous position against the Bridewell wall to protect them from the 'increase in traffic' generated by the newly-built Fire Station. A public subscription raised £27 to provide the lych-gate type structure against the churchyard wall.

◄ **THE STOCKS** *2004* O8724

A plaque on the structure protecting the stocks refers to the legislation of 1376, which required that stocks be set up in every town and village 'to encourage virtue and discourage evil doers'.

**ALL SAINTS' CHURCH** *1903* 49203

The former plaster on the external walls was removed by misguided restoration work in 1889, which has exposed the unknapped flint. This would have come from the local chalk downs, and the stone for the windows, tracery and doorways perhaps came from Bentley, some five miles to the south.

## ALL SAINTS' CHURCH, THE INTERIOR *1924* 75283

The organ (right) was moved from the north aisle to its present
position in 1908. The Jacobean oak pulpit of c1630 was found in
the tower arch covered in white paint, and was placed in its
present position during the restoration of the church in 1851.
Its elaborate carvings depict Aaron's rod and the scroll of the law.
During the Second World War it was stored for safe keeping in
Wookey Hole caves, Somerset. The painted glass east window was
installed in 1858 in memory of Lt Col C W Short, a veteran of
Waterloo. The Ten Commandments on the chancel wall were
repainted in 1907 by William Peskett, a plumber, painter and
glazier who lived in Bury Cottage.

**ALL SAINTS' CHURCH** *1903* 49202

The bold square brick tower was built onto a 13th-century base c1656 after an earlier tower had collapsed. The west doorway of the tower was remodelled in 1897 to mark Queen Victoria's Diamond Jubilee. The porch of the doorway on the south wall was removed about this time. Adjacent to it between the two windows are two pre-Reformation mass clocks; they are sundials, but their gnomons (the projecting part that casts the shadow) have long since disappeared. The brick and tile building on the right is known as the Pest House.

**ALL SAINTS' CHURCH FROM CHAMBERLAIN GARDENS** *2004* O8726

Chamberlain Gardens occupy part of the land given to the parish by the Misses Chamberlain, who lived at Bury House. On the left, the Vicarage was built in 1989-90. To the right, Benford Court was opened in 1980 and is part of the almshouse complex.

**THE PEST HOUSE** *2004* O8742

The Pest House was built c1622 by the churchwardens and overseers as a cottage for the poor on land given by Julian Smith, a linen draper. Believed to have housed people with infectious diseases in the 18th and 19th centuries, it was last occupied in the 1930s. By 1969 it was semi-derelict and subsequently threatened with demolition. Saved by a rescue committee, it was restored by the Odiham Society in 1981 and now houses a mini museum. It is owned by the Odiham Consolidated Charities.

### THE ALMSHOUSES *1903* 49211

Situated next to the Pest House and south of the church, this single-storey block of ten houses ranges on three sides of a courtyard. The almshouses were endowed in 1623 by Sir Edward More, lord of the manor of Odiham, which he leased from the Crown from 1587 to 1623.

**THE GATEWAY TO THE ALMSHOUSES** *1910* 63014

**THE GATEWAY TO THE ALMSHOUSES** *2004* O8710

**FROM THE CHURCH TOWER** *1906* 55851

In the foreground we see the roof of Bury House and its stables at the western end of The Bury. Facing south, Bury Villas are on the corner of Church Street (centre), which leads to the High Street. Diagonally opposite this junction stand the newly-built Palace Gate House and the farmhouse and buildings of Palace Gate Farm, next to the former deer park. Covering some 500 acres, the park was probably in existence in Saxon times; it was disparked and became farmland in the 17th century. To the west, The Priory, dated 1448-49 – a former rectory of the Chancellors of Salisbury, who were also rectors of Odiham – can be glimpsed through the trees. Nearer to the camera is the roof of The Close, a house dating from the 17th century.

## THE BURY *1910* 63009

Behind the railings (left), the 18th-century Bury House was owned by an attorney, John Cole, in the early 19th century. He built the adjacent office in part of his garden (the white porch on the right). On the opposite corner are the 16th-century Bury Villas; before the modern frontage was built they were one house, and jettied (with an overhanging upper storey). The left-hand house (on Church Street) was William Hole's baker's and confectioner's shop with an entrance from the front of the building. The bakery was situated in the yard behind. The Conservative Club (right) opened here in 1907 in the house built in 1781 by Benjamin Webb, a former headmaster of Odiham Grammar School. The 17th-century timber-framed Bell Inn next door was probably refronted at this time.

## THE BURY *2004*
O8718

There have been alterations to the façade of Bury House, which was home to the Misses Chamberlain from 1914 (they were the sisters of Neville Chamberlain, Prime Minister from 1937 to 1940). Webb House (formerly the Conservative Club, on the right) has now been divided into residential accommodation.

## THE BURY *c1955* O8018

Sydney Carter's butcher's shop occupied the cottage on the left from about 1914 to 1946. The 16th-century timber-framed jettied building next door, which in the late 17th century was owned by Robert May, a mercer and founder of the Grammar School, has been divided into two dwellings. The fine Georgian house in the centre has housed the telephone exchange since 1925, when it was moved from the post office at Mr Gotelee's shop in the High Street.

## THE BURY *2004*
O8719

The telephone exchange was moved from the Georgian house in the centre to a purpose-built building in the Farnham Road in 1967. The house was considerably altered c1975 by the addition of an extra storey, new windows and a doorcase to frame the front door. The white building in the distance – previously a shop – has had a former doorway blocked and another made into a window.

**THE BURY** *2004* O8737

Stoney Cottage, the jettied, timber-framed building on the left,
was saved from demolition and restored to one dwelling c1965.
In the distance, glimpsed on the right on the corner of King
Street, is the former forge, now a private house. Opposite, the
Oast Garage opened in the mid 1950s.

## THE GRAMMAR SCHOOL *1903* 49210

Opened in 1876, this new building by Edmund Woodthorpe RIBA replaced the original school, which was founded in 1694 by Robert May, a mercer of Odiham. His will bequeathed the sum of £600 for 'the Maintenance of a Free-School in the Town of Odiham for the Educating of Twenty Boys inhabiting within the Parish of Odiham forever'.

## THE HEADMASTER'S HOUSE, THE GRAMMAR SCHOOL *1924* 75285

Previously known as Odiham Free School or Endowed School, in 1880 it became Odiham Grammar School and then legally in 1909 Robert May's Grammar School. The picture shows the headmaster's house and garden. Since the garden is on two different levels, it provided an excellent venue for open-air theatrical productions by school pupils. In 1921 the ground and first floors of the house were converted to offices, staff rooms and a library.

**OLD HOUSES** *1903* 49205 ▶

These 'Old Houses' are in The Bury. The black door on the left of the early 16th-century Cottage in The Bury has 'John Hellis Builder' inscribed on it. He was employed during a restoration of the church in 1851, continuing a family business dating from the mid 17th century. Opposite, on the corner of King Street, Mrs Burrows was continuing a long-established blacksmith's business at the 16th-century forge. On the other side of King Street the sign advertises that P Cutmore, 'Fly and Omnibus Proprietor', operated from here. His horse-drawn vehicles provided a service to and from Winchfield Station, and he also delivered parcels.

▲ **THE BURY** *1910* 63010

The Fire Station and Parish Room on the left opened in 1904. The unusual 15th-century three-storey building (centre) is thought perhaps to have been a gatehouse to a former courtyard house, now Nos 67 and 69 High Street. The 19th-century hop kilns in the background formed part of King & Palmer's brewery in King Street, which was bought by Crowleys of Alton in 1895.

**THE BURY** *2004* O8720 ▶

The Fire Station which had stood on the left was demolished in 1966. The lower sash windows of the houses on the left have been replaced by casement windows, and their number increased. On the right, a doorway has been replaced by a window. The wooden, louvred box-like structures on the top of the hop kilns in King Street have disappeared.

► **OLD HOUSES,
CEMETERY HILL**
*1906* 53718

The 18th- and early 19th-century cottages on the left face the timber-framed house, which was built as a single dwelling in 1540; it is continuously jettied with a hearth-passage entrance, or in other words an internal chimney stack is positioned behind the entrance. By 1834, when it was known as Kings Barn Farm, it had been divided into three dwellings.

◄**CEMETERY HILL** *2004*
O8722

Much restoration work has taken place on the building on the right; it has been painted, and the attractive lattice windows have been replaced. The black paintwork enables better appreciation of the timber frame. It was restored to one dwelling with access through the original entrance in the mid 1960s, and renamed Tudor Cottages.

▲ **OLD HOUSES, CEMETERY HILL** *1910* 63011

In 1834, Kings Barn Farm (right) was part of the Tylney Hall estate. Part of the curtilage (the land belonging to it) became the cemetery, which gives this location its name. In 1910 the Old Houses were part of the curtilage of The Yews, now No 57 High Street. The view looks towards the High Street, down King Street.

◀**OLD HOUSES, CEMETERY HILL**
*1910* 63011

Detail.

**KING STREET** *2004* O8732

The side view of the former Kings Arms (which is now a restaurant) shows how the original wattle and daub infilling in the panels between the timber frame was replaced during the 1953 restoration using second-hand bricks. The ground floor outer wall was also rebuilt. Next door (right foreground) is Charlotte Terrace, which before its conversion to residential use in 1988 was the Assembly Rooms.

The old Assembly Rooms
~ now Charlotte Terrace

The Old House

# THE HIGH STREET AND THE CHALK PIT

**HIGH STREET** *c1965* O8054

The photograph captures the gentle curve of the High Street as it descends eastward. Manchester House, on the left, is a china and glassware shop. Next door, Kingston House has a Georgian façade built from the red brick made locally. It conceals a timber-framed building of medieval origins. Opposite, the former White Hart closed in 1961 and became a private house.

▶ **HIGH STREET**
*1924* 75276

The Tuns Hotel on the left advertises 'billiards and garage'; earlier in 1903 they also had 'good accommodation for tourists'. An inn since the early 18th century when it was the Three Tuns, it was rebuilt after a fire c1900. Opposite is Monks butcher's shop, where successive members of the Monk family have retailed meat since the mid 19th century. Next door is Presslee, a watchmaker and jeweller.

◀**HIGH STREET** *2004*
O8706

Pavements have been re-laid, and parking bays have enabled tree planting designed to soften the streetscape. The chemist moved from No 49 High Street to the shop on the left in 1967. Beyond (where the car is emerging) is a new road, Deer Park View, leading to the Health Centre, a car park and Red Lion Court. Opposite, the Old White Hart is now offices, and its former carriage entrance has been infilled to become a shop.

▲ **HIGH STREET** *c1950*  O8028

Next door to the White Hart (right) is Monks Cottage (named after Mrs Monk, a former resident), dated 1300. It was originally jettied (with an overhanging upper storey), and is the oldest known domestic building in the parish and one of the oldest in Hampshire.

◀**HIGH STREET** *1955*
O8042

The sign 'Luncheons and Teas' on the right, just beyond the White Hart, advertises the Two Sisters Café, which from 1939 to 1949 was also a guest house. Further on, the three-storey brick building has been a draper's shop for some 170 years; its name Commerce House records that this was where Odiham's first bank opened in 1806.

**THE GEORGE HOTEL AND HIGH STREET** *c1955*
O8041

Successive generations of the Dicker family have traded in the first shop on the left as grocers, wine and spirit merchants since 1857. The George Hotel next door has been an inn since at least 1585. Opposite, the tobacconist's sign is outside the sweet shop – another premises which has been in the same business for over 100 years.

**HIGH STREET,
LOWER END** *c1950* O8008

After conversion from the Fancy Repository into a garage in 1914, during the Second World War and until 1949 London House (left) became a British Restaurant. It is now divided into three shops, variously sweets, bicycles, a baker's, a cleaner's, a hairdresser's and a boutique. Mr Chapple opened his garage further down the street in 1914 – note the petrol pumps on the pavement – and on either side are a barber's shop and a café advertising teas.

**HIGH STREET** *1903* 49199

Mr Baker opened his Fancy Repository in London House (left) c1895. Next door, both the ivy-covered houses were owned by the local GP - the smaller one was used for a surgery. Further on, the white house was occupied by Mr Purkess, the grocer and provision merchant, who was also a baker. Opposite, the Kings Arms (near right), owned by Crowleys of Alton, a former merchant's house, was originally jettied on both street sides (see also page 36).

**HIGH STREET** *c1950* O8029

Removal of the ivy enables us to admire the late 18th-century
house (with a painter in action, left) and next door, a Georgian
façade conceals a timber-framed house dated to 1454-55.
Opposite, the Kings Arms has a new sign and is now owned by
Watneys. Next door, the Capital and Counties Bank moved here
in 1882 from the next house (after the gap), which was the
Hampshire Banking Co premises from c1849. Subsequently, in
the 1920s Leonard Campbell Taylor RA lived here. He was one of
six artists commissioned to paint the Coronation of George VI.

**HIGH STREET** *c1960* O8048

Pavements were installed prior to the Queen's visit to RAF
Odiham in 1953. The building housing Mr Chapple's garage was
demolished in 1952 and rebuilt, set back to provide a forecourt
(left). The Kings Arms (near right) was given a new look in 1953:
the old plaster was removed to expose the timber-framing, new
windows were installed, and the attractive porch was removed
(see also page 36).

**THE WAR MEMORIAL** *1924* 75278

The war memorial on Gospel Green, designed by the architect Morley Horder, was unveiled in 1920 by Viscount Wolmer MP. Odiham's first regular motor bus service – the Aldershot and District Traction Company's Daimler bus Service 7 from Aldershot – passed through Farnham, Crondall, Odiham and Hook to Basingstoke. Next to a former shop (where Charles Pither had sold china and glass and made picture frames between c1900 and 1910) is the entrance to the Congregational Chapel, built c1739. Adjacent to that is one of the High Street's 'new' houses, built in Queen Victoria's Diamond Jubilee year – 1897.

**HIGH STREET** *c1960* O8049

The first house on the left is a 16th-century timber-framed
structure with an early 17th-century façade. Next door, several
generations of the Hellis family, who were auctioneers, estate
agents, builders and carpenters, traded from here. Their builders'
yard at the rear was a former farmyard. The early 17th-century
house on the right has an 18th-century exterior. For some 100
years it was the residence of successive members of one family:
James Brooks came to Odiham in 1818 to join an attorney's
partnership, and his descendants continued as solicitors in a
purpose-built office in Church Street.

**HIGH STREET** *c1965*  O8068

The façade of the 18th-century Grey House on the left originally
resembled that of its neighbour. The Farnham Road (curving
gently to the right) has recently been widened, and a row of
poplar trees removed. The cottages are of different ages, but were
probably refronted c1800.

**HIGH STREET** *2004* O8721

In 1991the junction with London Road (to the left) was realigned in the interest of road safety, and a pedestrian refuge in the High Street was installed. London Road continues as Colt Hill and was truncated by the Odiham bypass, which was opened in 1981. There is now only pedestrian access to Odiham Common.

## THE LONDON AND FARNHAM ROADS *1908* 60089

Already licensed by the mid 18th century, the Angel Inn (left) stands at the junction of the High Street and London Road. The latter was a turnpike road for the Odiham, Hartley Wintney and Eversley Cross Trust. Mr R W Kail, baker, grocer and confectioner (centre) was continuing in the same business which had operated in these premises since c1828. Earlier, this had been the Half Moon and Punchbowl brew house and shop. The single-storey building at the rear is the former gatehouse of the Odiham and Farnham Turnpike Trust.

▲ **THE LONDON AND FARNHAM ROADS** *c1960* O8040

A pedestrian refuge has appeared at the junction of the London Road, which leads to Colt Hill, the Basingstoke Canal and Odiham Common. H W Thornton has taken over the long-established baker's, grocer's and confectioner's business on the corner.

◄ **FARNHAM ROAD** *2004* O8729

After some 170 years, Odiham has lost its bakery. However, planning legislation has ensured that the Hovis sign remains to remind future generations that there were local facilities here before the advent of the supermarket.

**HIGH STREET** *1908* 60087

Two plaster plaques on the wall of a first-floor room perhaps verify that prisoners from the Napoleonic Wars were lodged in the 17th-century cottage on the left. This is also an example of one of the many former single dwellings in the High Street that were divided in the early 19th century to meet the increased demand for housing. The road has now been sprayed with tar and then sanded to provide a better surface – a controversial experiment, which was paid for by the sister of the doctor who founded the local hospital – at a cost of £25!

▲ **HIGH STREET,** *The War Memorial c1955* O8044

The wide, gently curving High Street is perhaps best admired from its lowest point and looking west. The extension to the war memorial after the Second World War was designed by the architect C L Gill. His home, The White House (diagonally opposite) is a Grade II* listed building built in 1812 for a local banker. It is a fine and important example of an elegant town house.

**HIGH STREET** *1908* 60086

The listed Grade II* late 17th-century three-storey house on the left, with a magnificent carved shell hood over the doorcase, is Odiham's most splendid house. Since 1861 the residence of successive Medical Officers for Health, it is now occupied by Dr Davison. Next door is an 18th century building with three stone urns above the parapet. This has been a butcher's shop since c1847 and is now A J Parsons, a butcher's, fishmonger's and poulterer's.

**MARYCOURT'S ELABORATE ►
DOORCASE**

**MARYCOURT ►**

The Old House

**THE PILASTERED DOORCASE OF THE OLD HOUSE**

**HIGH STREET** *1906* 53714

The imposing red brick house of c1500 on the right (now The Old House and Queen Anne House) was a wealthy merchant's jettied house prior to its refronting and dividing in the 18th century. Further along is Waterloo House (with the blinds), where Miss Jenkins sold gloves and corsets in addition to her dressmaking and millinery business. Next door is Mr Purkess, a baker and grocer.

**HIGH STREET** *c1970* O8070

Considerable changes to the street frontage have occurred since
1906. The house on the right now has a bay window, and to its left
a former carriage entrance has been filled in to become Mrs
Holt's antique shop. Mr Chapples's garage has replaced Mr
Purkess's baker's and grocer's shop, which in 1952 was
demolished to create a garage forecourt.

**HIGH STREET** *c1955*  O8038

On the left is First Fruits, a greengrocer's, who also sell farm eggs, poultry and cream. In the three-storey building beyond, Mr N P Facy, draper, gents' outfitter, boots, shoes, ladies' and children's wear, is continuing the same line of business which has operated here continuously since c1784. Similarly, on the right is Hand Bros, an ironmonger's selling tools, guns and cartridges, brushes and paint, garden requisites, and wireless, and undertaking repairs of all kinds; they have been here for 35 years, continuing a business started in the 18th century.

**HIGH STREET** *c1950* O8007

W Fountain & Son, corn, coal and seed merchants, and the
Cherry Restaurant and Guest House (right) occupy a very fine but
much altered mid 16th-century building: a former courtyard
house named Walters, for nearly 350 years it was owned by
Corpus Christi College, Oxford. In the mid 19th century the right-
hand side housed the Mechanics Institute, where Charles
Kingsley, the author and nationally known supporter of social
reform, gave reading and writing lessons for 2d a week.

**HIGH STREET** *2004* O8714

The former ironmonger's shop became a building society office and is now an estate agent's. Next door, further alterations took place in the early 1980s to this historic building; converted to Fountains Mall, it was divided internally into individual shops.

**THE GEORGE HOTEL** *1924* 75277

Situated in the High Street, this late medieval courtyard inn dates from 1474, and before its restoration in the 18th century was jettied along its entire frontage. The date AD 1547 on the sign probably records new ownership. In 1544 Henry VIII had confiscated this property and the lands that went with it, and the owner (a Roman Catholic) was outlawed for high treason. The Petty Sessions were held here until 1882, and over the years the premises were also a posting house, a railway booking office and an Excise and Inland Revenue office. The inaugural meeting of the Odiham Society for Agriculture and Industry was held here in 1783. The initiative shown by this local society led to the formation of the Royal Veterinary Society. The last building on the same side of the road had been occupied since 1915 by Mr W Boyce, builder, plumber, house decorator and sanitary engineer, continuing the business started by Mr J J B Cooper c1850.

**HIGH STREET** *c1970* O8071

A pedestrian refuge is now in place. Halfway along on the right, the former Tuns Hotel closed in 1965, and downstairs has been converted into two shops: F J Auger, a clock repairer, and Swan and Cygnet Cleaners.

**HIGH STREET** *2004*
O8708

The pedestrian crossing was installed in the late 1970s. A former grocer's shop for over 200 years has become part of The George Hotel with a café downstairs. In the former Tuns Hotel the previous two shops have become one, a travel agent's.

**HIGH STREET** *1906* 53715

In addition to being postmaster at Odiham Post Office on the right, Mr Arthur Gotelee is Registrar of Births, Deaths and Marriages. He is also a bookseller, newsagent and stationer, and the business includes a printing works at the rear. Diagonally opposite, next to the White Hart, is the Terry family's grocery, provisions, bakery and confectionery business, which was established in 1875.

THE HIGH STREET AND THE CHALK PIT

▲ **THE WHITE HART INN AND HIGH STREET** *c1955*  O8043

The post office moved next door to the White Hart from the newsagent across the road in 1945. The last house on the right (which appears in the photograph showing The George in 1924 on pg. 60 and opposite) was destroyed by a bomb in 1940. Glimpsed through the trees is Palace Gate House, built in c1900.

◄ **HIGH STREET**
*2004*  O8731

These neo-Georgian houses built in 1995 replaced Palace Gate House, which was demolished c1987 as part of the development for housing of the last working farm in Odiham. Palace Gate was the site of a former manor house – Odiham Place.

**THE VICARAGE** *1924* 75284

It is unusual that the vicarage in the High Street is built to a very high standard and size, a reflection perhaps on the wealth of this large and prosperous parish. Originally an open medieval hall, it dates from 1395-96.

**THE OLD VICARAGE** *2004* O8711

The former extensive porch and the eastern wing were probably
removed in 1927-28 when major alterations took place. The
property passed into private ownership, and the new vicarage
adjacent to the church was built in 1990.

**THE PRIORY,** *the Remains of the Old Guest House 1906* 53717

The title 'Old Guest House' may refer to the building which housed visiting clergy before 1856, when this was the rectory of the Chancellors of Salisbury, the patrons of All Saints' Church. It was renamed when it passed into private hands. The large partly ruinous chamber block dates to 1448-49.

**WESTERN CROSS**
*2004* O8713

The former toll house was demolished as part of a road-widening scheme, and access to and from West Street was blocked to traffic in the interest of safety. In the 1950s and 1960s, The Radio House of Odiham, selling electrical appliances, TV and radio, occupied the former shop, which has now been converted to a private house.

## HIGH STREET *1908*  60088

Western Cross is the junction of the High Street, Alton Road, Dunleys Hill and West Street. On the left is the former toll house of the Basingstoke, Odiham and Alton Turnpike Trust, established in 1736. William Nash's premises (left), a boot and shoemaker who is also a postman, fronts onto West Street, formerly called Pound Lane. Aaron Cooper, a clock and watchmaker on the opposite corner, was continuing his father's trade. The entrance gates of The Priory are on the right.

**THE CHALK PIT** *1903* 49208

This view, looking north towards the entrance (in the Alton
Road), shows several cottages built of chalk, some of which have
since been demolished. They were built c1800, reputedly to
house French prisoners of the Napoleonic wars, who were on
parole in Odiham. The building with the tall chimneys fronts the
Alton Road, and is built into the cliff of the chalk pit. Dating from
c1730, it was originally a beer house, the Sign of the Castle.

**THE CHALK PIT** *1910* 63017

Covering some eight acres, this is believed to be the largest chalk pit in Hampshire. In addition to providing lime, the chalk was used for marling the clay agricultural lands to the north and the sandy soils to the east. It is owned by the lord of the manor.

**THE CHALK PIT**
*2004* O8715

The former thatched building on the left now has a tiled roof. There is no public access to the chalk pit today.

69

# COLT HILL, THE BASINGSTOKE CANAL & WHITEHALL

**COLT HILL** *1911* 63020

From the eastern end of the High Street, London Road continues as Colt Hill. The sign on the house behind the children advertises W Clark & Sons, Carpenter & Undertaker. Next door are Mays Model Cottages, built in 1862 by a philanthropic local wine and spirit merchant. The New Inn (its sign is on a white post in the distance) in the 17th century was called the Lower House. The rent from it was held in trust to benefit the poor inhabitants of Odiham and Hartley Wintney, by annually providing canvas for shirts.

▲ **THE WHARF** *1908* 60090

We are looking west, with the Great Wharf of the Basingstoke Canal on the left. The roof of the New Inn can be seen through the trees (left); next to it is Wharf House, built in 1815 as the wharfinger's residence by the Company of Proprietors of the Basingstoke Canal. Adjoining the bridge is the Cricketers, owned by Crowleys of Alton, which closed as a public house the year the photograph was taken.

◄ **THE WHARF** *2004* O8744

This detail shows The Bridge House, formerly the Cricketers

▶ **THE BASINGSTOKE CANAL** *c1965* O8065

By 1920 the Cricketers, adjacent to Colt Hill bridge, was renamed The Bridge House. Its original name recorded the proximity of the Odiham and Greywell Club, whose ground on Odiham Common lay just over the bridge

◄ **THE CANAL WHARF** *1906*
55854

Behind the Cricketers, a warehouse and stables adjacent to the Little Wharf were rebuilt in 1815 after a fire. There were coal pens in the vicinity, as successive landlords were also coal merchants. From c1890 the premises was advertised as the Cricketers Inn and Boating House.

**THE BASINGSTOKE CANAL** *c1965* O8064

The photograph shows Colt Hill Bridge and the rear of The Bridge House. In 1949 the New Basingstoke Canal Company bought the canal from the Harmsworth family, who had owned it since 1923. Under new ownership there was no commercial traffic, and the canal had become derelict by the time of this photograph.

**THE VIEW FROM CANAL BRIDGE** *1924* 75279

The winding hole (where boats are turned) lies to the east of and adjacent to the Great Wharf. Odiham Common is on the northern bank. The canal turns to the north-east before reaching Broad Oak Bridge.

**WHITEHALL** *1910*
63019

This small hamlet of Whitehall lies across Odiham Common; it housed mainly families whose menfolk worked in the nearby brickworks on the common, which closed in 1907. Successive generations of the Nevill family were employed there for over 100 years. The thatched cottages nearest the camera have long since been demolished.

**PILLARS BRIDGE ON THE CANAL** *1903* 49212

This bridge linked long-established footpaths crossing Dogmersfield Park to Odiham Common; they had become divided by the construction of the Basingstoke Canal. The bridge became derelict, and was demolished in the late 1920s.

# THE SURROUNDING VILLAGES
## NORTH WARNBOROUGH, GREYWELL, DOGMERSFIELD AND LONG SUTTON

▲ **NORTH WARNBOROUGH,** *The Village 1904* 51324

From Odiham, Dunleys Hill leads to North Warnborough. The two houses on the left of the road to Hook were part of a flourishing nursery business which occupied the land behind them in the 18th and 19th centuries. Opposite, the Methodist chapel was opened in 1895. George Prior was the sub-postmaster, grocer and baker at the shop facing the pond.

◄ **NORTH WARNBOROUGH,** *Priors Corner 2004* N198702

Considerable changes have taken place as part of the road widening and realignment of c1950. Although now a roundabout, it is still known as Priors Corner, recording the former shopkeeper's name. The houses beyond the office complex, Alexandra Terrace, were built in 1906 by Alfred Girle, a local builder. They are named after the then Queen and his own daughter.

▲ **NORTH WARNBOROUGH**
*The Village 1904* 51325

The plastered section of this long building was known as Webbs Cottages, and the southern range, Portsmouth Cottages. The first one of the latter was the Reading Room and Club. Newspapers, magazines and a library were available to members, and they could also play billiards, darts and whist. Opposite, George Millam was using the osiers growing on the Green behind his cottage (built of chalk) in his trade as a basket maker. John Nevill started his baker's and grocer's business in c1840 in the cottage behind the horse and trap.

▲ **NORTH WARNBOROUGH,** *The Village 2004* N198703

This long row of jettied timber-framed buildings (now known as Castlebridge Cottages) is unusual in a rural setting. The central bay was destroyed at some time and has been rebuilt. The nearer range has been dendrodated to 1447-48, and the further to 1533-34. Only the first chimney of the nearer range is original, indicating domestic usage; this suggests that the rest of the building may have been connected with the local cloth industry which flourished in the 15th and 16th centuries. Road widening and drainage works resulted in the demolition of the cottage on the bend. The modern white gabled houses in the distance, Swan Mews, were built in 1995.

**NORTH WARNBOROUGH**
*The Jolly Miller*
*c1955* N198002

The Jolly Miller originally fronted the pavement in line with the cottages beyond. It was rebuilt in 1908 to plans by the architect Arthur J Stedman of Farnham in the mock-Tudor style prevalent at that time. The long range of dwellings – now called Castlebridge Cottages – was heavily 'restored' in the 1930s.

**NORTH WARNBOROUGH**
*The Jolly Miller 2004* N198705

**NORTH WARNBOROUGH**
*The Whitewater*
*1906* 55855

The River Whitewater rises at Bidden off the Upton Grey road, and here flows north-eastwards through the former deer park. It follows the road to Lodge Farm. The bypass, which opened in 1981, necessitated the realignment of this road from the new roundabout.

**NORTH WARNBOROUGH,** *Mill Corner c1955* N198001

Adjacent to the former King's Mill, the lane leads via the Green to the ford of the River Whitewater. From there a footpath leads to Odiham Castle. The formerly thatched 17th-century house on the right of the photograph was the Smith Brothers' coal merchant's business.

**NORTH WARNBOROUGH** *Mill Corner 2004* N198701

The old thatched cottage in the centre of the earlier picture was replaced by a modern house in the late 1970s, and the neighbouring house has been extended. A one-way traffic system is now in place.

**NORTH WARNBOROUGH,** *King John's Castle 1903*
49209

Odiham Castle, situated in a bend of the River Whitewater in
North Warnborough, is the only castle in England with an
octagonal keep. The construction of the Basingstoke Canal in
1794 cut through the castle's outer defences to the south.

**NORTH WARNBOROUGH,** *King John's Castle*
*2004* N198723

This whole area is now somewhat overgrown, making access
difficult, and the remains are more ruinous. A recent grant from
the Heritage Lottery Fund will enable Hampshire County
Council, under the guidance of English Heritage, to carry out
repairs, survey the site, improve access and increase public
awareness of this historic site.

**GREYWELL,** *The Church of St Mary the Virgin 1904*
51319

The view shows the north side of the church, which dates from the late 12th century, and the fine Norman doorway. The 17th-century tower contains four bells. It is unusual that the rood-screen and loft are still in place – the rood loft is one of the two in Hampshire that survived the Reformation.

**GREYWELL,** *The Village 1903* 49213

These are typical of many of the cottages in Greywell, which were plastered and painted white at this time. In the early to mid 19th century Mrs Wigley kept a post office in one of these cottages.

**GREYWELL**
*The Village*
*2004* G61701

The 16th-century timber-framed Cedar Cottages are barely recognisable as the same ones in No 49213, above, now that the plaster has been removed and they have been converted to a terrace. In contrast, Cedar House has been painted white.

▶ **GREYWELL**
*The Fox and Goose*
*1908* 60091

James Paine, the
landlord, stands on
the forecourt in his
shirtsleeves. Manorial
court dinners were
held at the Sign of The
Fox in the early 19th
century. The
cartsheds and shop of
William White, a
carter and
shopkeeper, stand on
the corner of
Deptford Lane and
the road to Hook
Common.

◀ **GREYWELL,** *Greywell Hill*
*1903* 49215

Built on the side of a hill, Greywell
Hill was purchased in 1787 by the 1st
Lord Dorchester, formerly Sir Guy
Carleton, who was the first Governor
General of Canada. He bought the
manors of Greywell and Nately
Scures from the trustees of the Earl of
Northington. A considerable number
of possible male heirs died fighting
for king/queen and country, and the
title became extinct. However, as a
result of petitioning, Queen Victoria
recreated the title in the female
heiress, but it became extinct again in
1963. Greywell Hill is now the
residence of the 7th Earl of
Malmesbury, whose mother was the
daughter of the 2nd Baron Dorchester.

▲ **GREYWELL,** *The Malthouse 2004* G61703

This is a very fine 16th-century house which appears to have had non-domestic use, perhaps as a manorial court-house, before its conversion to a dwelling. Several maltsters lived here in the 18th century, and before 1928 there were two hop kilns next door.

◄**DOGMERSFIELD**
*Dogmersfield House
1903* 49216

Built on the site of a palace of the Bishop of Bath and Wells, the present house dates from 1728. It was built by the lord of the manor of Dogmersfield, Ellis St John, and remained as the St John/Mildmay residence until 1933.

**LONG SUTTON,** *The Village 1904* 51320

The house on the left is the residence of the headmaster of the adjoining school, opposite the church. All Saints' Church, dating from the 13th century, is a small roughcast building with an old tiled roof. The grey wooden turret with three bells is supported in the nave by four posts.

# INDEX

# BIBLIOGRAPHY

*Odiham High Street - an Itinerary.* The Odiham Society 2003

S Millard: *The Parish of Odiham – an Historical Guide.* The Odiham Society 1993

P A L Vine: *London's Lost Route to Basingstoke.* Alan Sutton Publishing Ltd 1994

D Spruce: *The Church in the Bury.* Odiham Parochial Church Council 2001

P MacGregor: *Odiham Castle 1200-1500.* Alan Sutton Publishing Ltd 1983

P Holmes: *Odiham Grammar School.* 1991

E Roberts: *Hampshire Houses 1250-1700.* Hampshire County Council 2003

# NAMES OF SUBSCRIBERS

The following people have kindly supported this book by subscribing to copies before publication.

A. S. M. & J. K. Anderson

Mr Eric Baker

John & Eileen Baker, Odiham

David Barnacle

James Barnacle

Kate Barnacle

Ray Bassett

The Beach Family, Odiham

The Bennett Family, Odiham

Ruth Bever

Mr & Mrs A. P. Bone

Fred & Maureen Brailey

Paul, Theresa, Madisen & Averi Brailey

Martin & Nicola Brindley 6th May 2000

Roger, Sheila, Simon, Rachel Buck, North Warnborough

The Bunting Family

Mr R. & Mrs M. Butchers

In Memory of Grandad 'Cameron'

Laurie Carey

Sonia Carter

In Memory of Odiham, K. J. Chapman

The Collingborn Family

David Collins

James Cooke's Family, Hartley Wintney

Dorothy A. Crocker

Remembering Millicent Crook (nee Wooldridge)

Elizabeth & Jason Cross

G. J. Cruikshank, Odiham

The Family of William Crumplin, Odiham

Dave & Lynn Curtin, Odiham

Mr N. S. J. Curtin

The Drayton Family

Mrs D. H. M. Dyson

George Elliott & Eileen Elliott

Elaine Fairless, Teddington

Avery Fathers

John Fletcher, Forge House, Odiham

Mr M. F. & Mrs S. M. Forrester

Anthony Fountain

Peter Fountain

The Galliver Family

In Memory of Sandra Gepp (nee Turnbull)

Anthony H. C. Gepp

Liz & Ian Gornall

The Haines Family, Greenhill, Odiham

Wesley Harper

Walter Roy Hedges

The Heywood Family, Odiham

Chris Hogben, Old Bank House, Odiham

Mr D. J. Jordan & Mrs W. Jordan

Pauline M. Joy

The Keens Family

Peter & Moira Kelsey

Sara A. Kimber

David & Carol Kirkpatrick, Odiham

The Knight Family, Odiham

John & Carol Lambert, Reyntiens View

The Laycock Family

J. A. Lee

K. H. Lee

Paul & Sue Luker and Family

Sir Nevil & Lady Macready, Odiham

The Earl of Malmesbury

The Marais Families

David Marshall, Truro

Bill & Susie Mathers

Mayhill Junior School, Odiham

David Mitchell

Peter & Patricia Moore

The Oliver Family, Odiham

Jack & Kay Ormerod

Topsy Osbon

Gillian & Tony Paine, Odiham, Hampshire

Ray Perks

James & Jennifer Peskett

Judy Phillips, Hook

Rosina Grace Lee Phillips Cawley

Mr & Mrs E. A. Pither, Odiham

Ella May Porter, Hook, Hants

Keith E. Porter, Odiham

Pamela Porter

Geoffrey R. Potten, Odiham 2004

David Pratt & Sylvia Pratt

John Pratt & Jane Pratt

Sir Humphrey Prideaux

Simon Quarrell

Jane Quarry

The Radmann Family

The Read Family, Odiham

J. & E. Robinson-Giannasi

Alan Robson, Odiham

For Christine Sillers and her Odiham ancestors

Greta R. Simmonds, Hook, Hampshire

Mr P. & Mrs T. Skinner, Charlotte Terrrace

Dorothy Mary Smith

Lesley & Terence Spencer

Alan & Marion Spruce

Mr C. O. Steer, Newbury

Bob & Pam Steward, North Warnborough

John Hilton Steward, North Warnborough

Swalheim

June & John Tinsley

Christopher & Sylvia Tofts

Valerie Trowbridge

Mary Turvill

Pauline Twineham, Odiham - 2004

Edward Stuart Wardle, Odiham

Jonathan Charles Wardle, Odiham

Richard Ian Wardle, Odiham

Ian Williams & Tracy Williams, Odiham

The Williams Family,
Odiham & North Warnborough

Anne & Oliver Willmore, Odiham

Alan & Linda Wood, Odiham

Martin & Jane Woods

J. H. Van Wyngaarden

# FRITH PRODUCTS & SERVICES

Francis Frith would doubtless be pleased to know that the pioneering publishing venture he started in 1860 still continues today. Over a hundred and forty years later, The Francis Frith Collection continues in the same innovative tradition and is now one of the foremost publishers of vintage photographs in the world. Some of the current activities include:

## Interior Decoration

Today Frith's photographs can be seen framed and as giant wall murals in thousands of pubs, restaurants, hotels, banks, retail stores and other public buildings throughout the country. In every case they enhance the unique local atmosphere of the places they depict and provide reminders of gentler days in an increasingly busy and frenetic world.

## Product Promotions

Frith products are used by many major companies to promote the sales of their own products or to reinforce their own history and heritage. Frith promotions have been used by Hovis bread, Courage beers, Scots Porage Oats, Colman's mustard, Cadbury's foods, Mellow Birds coffee, Dunhill pipe tobacco, Guinness, and Bulmer's Cider.

## Genealogy and Family History

As the interest in family history and roots grows world-wide, more and more people are turning to Frith's photographs of Great Britain for images of the towns, villages and streets where their ancestors lived; and, of course, photographs of the churches and chapels where their ancestors were christened, married and buried are an essential part of every genealogy tree and family album.

## Frith Products

All Frith photographs are available Framed or just as Mounted Prints and Posters (size 23 x 16 inches). These may be ordered from the address below. From time to time other products - Address Books, Calendars, Table Mats, etc - are available.

## The Internet

Already fifty thousand Frith photographs can be viewed and purchased on the internet through the Frith websites and a myriad of partner sites.

For more detailed information on Frith companies and products, look at these sites:

www.francisfrith.co.uk
www.francisfrith.com
*(for North American visitors)*

See the complete list of Frith Books at:

*www.francisfrith.co.uk*

This web site is regularly updated with the latest list of publications from the Frith Book Company. If you wish to buy books relating to another part of the country that your local bookshop does not stock, you may purchase on-line.

*For further information, trade, or author enquiries please contact us at the address below:*
**The Francis Frith Collection, Frith's Barn, Teffont, Salisbury, Wiltshire, England SP3 5QP.**
Tel: +44 (0)1722 716 376  Fax: +44 (0)1722 716 881  Email: sales@francisfrith.co.uk

# See Frith books on the internet at www.francisfrith.co.uk

# FREE MOUNTED PRINT

**Mounted Print**
*Overall size 14 x 11 inches*

**Fill in and cut out this voucher and return**
*it with your remittance for £2.25 (to cover postage and handling). Offer valid for delivery to UK addresses only.*

**Choose any photograph included in this book.**
*Your SEPIA print will be A4 in size. It will be mounted in a cream mount with a burgundy rule line (overall size 14 x 11 inches).*

**Order additional Mounted Prints at HALF PRICE (only £7.49 each*)**
If you would like to order more Frith prints from this book, possibly as gifts for friends and family, you can buy them at half price (with no additional postage and handling costs).

**Have your Mounted Prints framed**
For an extra £14.95 per print* you can have your mounted print(s) framed in an elegant polished wood and gilt moulding, overall size 16 x 13 inches (no additional postage and handling required).

---

**\* IMPORTANT!**

**These special prices are only available if you order at the same time as you order your free mounted print. You must use the ORIGINAL VOUCHER on this page (no copies permitted). We can only despatch to one address.**

---

*Send completed Voucher form to:*
**The Francis Frith Collection, Frith's Barn, Teffont, Salisbury, Wiltshire SP3 5QP**

# CHOOSE ANY IMAGE FROM THIS BOOK

## *Voucher* for **FREE** and Reduced Price Frith Prints

*Please do not photocopy this voucher. Only the original is valid, so please fill it in, cut it out and return it to us with your order.*

| Picture ref no | Page no | Qty | Mounted @ £7.49 | Framed + £14.95 | Total Cost |
|---|---|---|---|---|---|
| | | 1 | Free of charge* | £ | £ |
| | | | £7.49 | £ | £ |
| | | | £7.49 | £ | £ |
| | | | £7.49 | £ | £ |
| | | | £7.49 | £ | £ |
| | | | £7.49 | £ | £ |
| *Please allow 28 days for delivery* | | | * Post & handling (UK) | | £2.25 |
| | | | **Total Order Cost** | | £ |

Title of this book . . . . . . . . . . . . . . . . . . . . . . . .

I enclose a cheque/postal order for £ . . . . . . . . . .
made payable to 'The Francis Frith Collection'

OR please debit my Mastercard / Visa / Switch / Amex card
*(credit cards please on all overseas orders),* **details below**

Card Number

Issue No (Switch only)        Valid from (Amex/Switch)

Expires        Signature

Name   Mr/Mrs/Ms ..........................................

Address ..........................................
..........................................
..........................................
.......................... Postcode ..................

Daytime Tel No ..........................................

Email ..........................................

Valid to 31/12/05

**Would you like to find out more about Francis Frith?**

We have recently recruited some entertaining speakers who are happy to visit local groups, clubs and societies to give an illustrated talk documenting Frith's travels and photographs. If you are a member of such a group and are interested in hosting a presentation, we would love to hear from you.

Our speakers bring with them a small selection of our local town and county books, together with sample prints. They are happy to take orders. A small proportion of the order value is donated to the group who have hosted the presentation. The talks are therefore an excellent way of fundraising for small groups and societies.

**Can you help us with information about any of the Frith photographs in this book?**

We are gradually compiling an historical record for each of the photographs in the Frith archive. It is always fascinating to find out the names of the people shown in the pictures, as well as insights into the shops, buildings and other features depicted.

If you recognize anyone in the photographs in this book, or if you have information not already included in the author's caption, do let us know. We would love to hear from you, and will try to publish it in future books or articles.

**Our production team**

Frith books are produced by a small dedicated team at offices in the converted Grade II listed 18th-century barn at Teffont near Salisbury, illustrated above. Most have worked with the Frith Collection for many years. All have in common one quality: they have a passion for the Frith Collection. The team is constantly expanding, but currently includes:

Paul Baron, Jason Buck, John Buck, Ruth Butler, Heather Crisp, David Davies, Isobel Hall, Julian Hight, Peter Horne, James Kinnear, Karen Kinnear, Tina Leary, Stuart Login, David Marsh, Sue Molloy, Glenda Morgan, Wayne Morgan, Kate Rotondetto, Dean Scource, Eliza Sackett, Terence Sackett, Sandra Sampson, Adrian Sanders, Sandra Sanger, Julia Skinner, Claire Tarrier, Lewis Taylor, Shelley Tolcher, Lorraine Tuck and Jeremy Walker.